T0328748

# DISCIPLINA

# CAMBRIDGE
## UNIVERSITY PRESS

University Printing House, Cambridge CB2 8BS, United Kingdom

Cambridge University Press is part of the University of Cambridge.

It furthers the University's mission by disseminating knowledge in the pursuit of
education, learning and research at the highest international levels of excellence.

www.cambridge.org
Information on this title: www.cambridge.org/9781107495104

© Cambridge University Press 1926

First published 1926
First paperback edition 2015

*A catalogue record for this publication is available from the British Library*

ISBN 978-1-107-49510-4 Paperback

# DISCIPLINA

BY

## W. H. S. JONES, Litt.D.

*Bursar of S. Catharine's College, Cambridge;*
*Bursar and Lecturer, Cambridge Training*
*College for Schoolmasters; once Senior*
*Classical Master at the Perse*
*School*

CAMBRIDGE

AT THE UNIVERSITY PRESS

MCMXXVI

TO
F. M. R.

## PREFACE

ONE who for nearly twenty-five years taught in secondary schools cannot find a better summary of the lesson impressed upon him there than a few sentences from a work of W. J. Long:

There, as with children, the first and strongest instinct of every creature is that of obedience. The essential difference between the two, between the human and the little wild animal, is this: the animal's one idea, born in him and strengthened by every day's training, is that, until he grows up and learns to take care of himself, his one business in the world is to be watchful for orders and to obey them instantly; while the child, by endless pettings and indulgences, by having every little cry attended to and fussed over as if it were a Caesar's mandate, too often loses the saving instinct of obedience and grows up into the idea that his business in the world is to give orders for others to obey. So that at three or five and twenty years, when the mischief is done, we must begin to teach the obedience which should never have been lost, and without which life is a worse than useless thing.

When one turns to the animals, it is often with the wholesome, refreshing sense that here is a realm where the law of life is known and obeyed. To the wild creature obedience is everything. It is the deep, unconscious tribute of ignorance to wisdom, of weakness to power....And one who watches the process with sympathetic eyes...can only wonder and grow thoughtful, and mend his crude theories of instinct and heredity by what he sees....

Tenderness and patience are here too, and the young are never driven beyond their powers....One thing more: these interesting little wild kindergartens are, emphatically, happy gatherings. The more I watch them, teachers and pupils, the more I long for some measure of their freedom, their strength of play, their joyfulness[1].

The question suggests itself: Why are obedience and happiness associated among the lower animals and dissociated among human beings? Why has the new principle of education, which bids us "follow the child," been no more successful than the old system founded on fear and repression?

I have tried to give an answer in this little book, which, whatever its faults, is the outcome of my own failures and disappointments. Any truth it contains was learnt by suffering.

It has not been my object to discuss the curriculum, the training of teachers, teaching and learning, and so on, at any length. I have merely tried to show how these parts of educational theory are connected with my conception of *disciplina*.

I have intentionally limited my remarks to secondary education (with occasional references to the University) and to boys. Nothing has been discussed of which I have not had a long personal experience, and so I rarely refer to

[1] *School of the Woods*, pp. 14–18.

primary education and never to the training of girls.

I hope that critics will criticise, not the faulty exposition of my thesis, but the thesis itself, which is just this: *Although the development of interest in subjects themselves is of great educational importance, the development of life purposes, to which separate interests are subordinated, is of much greater importance. Interest alone may enable us to learn (say) French; something more is required as the foundation of a good character.* It should be remembered that in practice a mere liking is often mistaken for a genuine interest.

I wish to thank my colleagues, Mr C. Fox, Mr R. S. Williamson, and Mr Roy Meldrum, for many corrections and for invaluable criticism.

W. H. S. J.

# CONTENTS

## CHAPTER ONE

*Introduction*

*Discipline and* disciplina

THIS little book is a protest to educators against the modern doctrine of "do as you please." It is at the same time a plea that they will lay a little less stress on interest, and a little more on the fighting spirit, the will to win the battle between the higher self and the lower.

When a young teacher is for the first time in front of his class, the sheer necessity of keeping order brings out plainly, albeit in a crude way, one essential factor in education. The foundation of his work, upon which depends the stability of all the superstructure, lies in the truth that the teacher must be, in the fullest and deepest sense of the word, a master. His will must be law. Any theory of education that assumes a fundamental postulate opposed to this is doomed to failure.

A logical proof of the dogmatic statements in the preceding paragraph is neither necessary nor possible. Only experience can show up the evil which inevitably follows when boys are allowed to have their own way, when their lower selves, in the absence of a master mind, become the dominating factor in the school or in the class-room. To say this is not to imply that boy-nature is essentially bad, nor that the master ought to be a domineering tyrant. Fear and repression are not the only weapons in his armoury. Sympathy and understanding will go much further than such deterrents in securing power of leadership, without which he cannot hope to succeed. But it is implied that we are the heirs of a possession won by toil and suffering; that we ought no more to let this go than we would carelessly lose a material inheritance; that in the nature of the case a boy cannot appreciate this inheritance, but is under the influence of his crude and often animal instincts; that he must be brought to see his true interest, and trained by habituation to achieve it. The conflict is not between his own wishes and those of his elders; it is between his lower and his higher self, between the pleasure of the moment and the realisation of an ideal. It is the teacher's first and supreme duty to see that this struggle is carried to a victorious issue. Many educationists maintain that, given a suitable environment, boys can be trusted to develop the best that is within them if allowed a free hand. This is a half-truth which has done incalculable harm to the cause of education. What is meant by a "suitable environment"? If it be a purely passive thing, it cannot produce the result we all desire; but if beside its passive merits it contains some active uplifting force, some compelling personality, then the contention that a suitable environment is sufficient for the best possible development may be accepted as true.

Life, for which education is, or should be, a preparation, is a struggle, an upward struggle towards something higher and better. It is not the gratification of the interest of the moment; it is not the elimination of the unpleasant. All education based, consciously or unconsciously, upon this elimination is bound to end in disaster. Teachers of all grades must resist the attractive but insidious forms in which the doctrine presents itself—interest, self-determination or what not. Pleasure, interest, self-determination, are all good things, and in their highest sense[1] may represent the supreme goal of human endeavour; if, however, we take their lower manifestations as our educational aim, we are going backwards instead of forwards. A lofty purpose, to which our immediate desires are strictly subordinated, is essential for all progress, whether in school life or in the world. Education is a fraud unless it not only sets forth clearly such purposes, but also develops in the minds of the scholars a feeling towards them which may be summed up in the two words "I must." The compelling influence

[1] I refer to the feeling of satisfaction that comes from successfully trying to do our best.

of the categorical imperative, commonly called
a sense of duty, is a factor without which education is not only useless but dangerous.

But the feeling "I must" rarely grows by itself; usually, if not always, it springs out of "thou
shalt." This is the reason why a teacher should
also be a master. He it is who by his influence
turns "thou shalt" into "I must"; in other
words he changes an external discipline into a
discipline from within. His work should be
judged by his success or failure to effect this
change.

The view here put forward is not retrograde[1];
it is not content, as the old schoolmaster was
content, with an external discipline. Nor does
it demand too much from boy-nature; it merely
insists that every scholar shall consciously and
intelligently do his best, in all his activities, with
a higher purpose than the immediate gratification of his likes and dislikes. On the other hand,
a protest is made against all extremists among
modern educationists who have reacted so far
from their predecessors that for "thou shalt"
they have substituted "do as thou wishest."

In brief, a plea is put forward that education
should result in enlightened self-discipline. To
say this is not to define education, nor to limit

[1] The retrograde policy is to allow children to do "as they
please." This is to employ the crudest methods of evolution,
which are quite out of place in education.

its scope and function; but a rule or standard is given whereby educational management may be tested and guided. This short preface should be regarded as a preliminary warning that a first principle will govern all subsequent discussion of the aims of education, of its methods, and of the forces that control it.

Discipline has been defined as the training of the will. How far this definition is correct may be seen from an examination of discipline in one of its simplest forms, that of military training.

The fundamental principle underlying military discipline is the subordination of individual wills to one controlling will. Its essential factors are implicit obedience and constant practice. Behind these lies some powerful emotion, which is not without an element of not necessarily dishonourable fear. In certain matters blind and unintelligent obedience is demanded; in others scope is given for the exercise of ingenuity and for the adaptation of means to a given end. In all forms of discipline we find these factors: subordination, obedience, practice, emotional stimulus, and more or less scope for initiative.

Discipline, then, is more than the training of the will. It is the merging of self-will in the social will, and the turning of a part of the self into a machine. In return for the sacrifice of his self-will the individual finds satisfaction for his social needs; and his becoming in part a machine frees his will from distractions and permits it to concentrate on the more important tasks of life.

The justification of discipline is its necessity. Without discipline any society—even a society of anarchists—must fall to pieces, and no aim requiring concentration of effort can be achieved. Discipline is in itself un-moral; morality enters the question only when the ethical value of the object in view is taken into account. "Good" discipline is effective discipline, "bad" discipline is discipline which fails in its purpose.

The coercion of discipline comes partly from without and partly from within. All "good" discipline tends to develop an internal restraint out of an external one—the motive force of the discipline rises gradually to a more spiritual level— and in this way is evolved one form of self-discipline. Self-discipline thus occurs when the individual organises the various habits, impulses, and desires of which his personality is composed into a unity under one will, with the lower parts restrained for the greater liberty of the higher.

The efficacy of discipline depends largely upon the degree of compulsion employed. The beautiful drill of a regiment of Guards is made possible only by the strict methods adopted to secure it, and a college boat will hardly improve its place on the river if training rules may be ignored. But there are many kinds of compulsion, and the strongest are often those behind which the physical constraint is the weakest. Shylock did not realise this when he asked:

On what compulsion must I? Tell me that

But Portia knew better. She knew the power of the instinct to show mercy, but also that this instinct must be felt before the force can manifest itself. So too there is no compulsion of a physical kind to make the martyr cleave to his convictions, or the mother sacrifice herself for her child. Yet conscience and mother-love have a driving force which will work miracles.

These spiritual forces are not without their element of fear, though it is refined and sublimated into the noble fear of falling short of one's best; it is the dread of feeling shame before one's self. But their truest ally is enlightenment. The deeper the insight into reality, the clearer the understanding of the consequences of one's acts, the greater the intelligence of the agent, so much the firmer will be the devotion and so much the more useful will be its exercise. The ignorant mother is deprived of many ways of showing her love, which is therefore correspondingly dwarfed and starved; she may also do her child positive harm by stupid actions. The martyr, again, if his convictions be not enlightened by understanding, becomes merely a "conscientious objector."

We see then that the compelling power of a

spiritual force is greatly increased by enlightenment. It reaches its maximum when this enlightenment includes a comprehension of the
moral ideal at which discipline aims. Ignorant
mother-love will make mistakes. Intelligent
mother-love may rear a bad citizen. But a love
reinforced by both intelligence and moral insight cannot fail to mould the character of a
child into the best form of which he is capable.

The best discipline is that exercised by a spiritual force, and the best spiritual force is one
enlightened by intelligence and moral insight.
It is because the English word "discipline" has
associations which over-estimate the element of
restraint, and under-estimate the elements of intelligence and morality which ought to be the
basis of that restraint, that I have chosen the
Latin word *disciplina* to denote what I take to
be the chief function of an educator. All that
uplifts a man is included in that term, and it
emphasises the often-forgotten truth that training and learning are essentially one.

Concentration, restraint of disturbing factors,
obedience to law, are not sufficient for progress;
they are merely the machinery with which the
progressive spirit works. To appreciate this truth
is to understand why progress brings with it two
apparently incompatibles—better discipline and
greater liberty. Men will not neglect, if they are
wise, the machine which has enabled them to

advance, and the advance itself brings with it wider scope for the exercise of initiative. Discipline and liberty are complementary; *disciplina* and progress are almost identical.

Certain factors in discipline are static. It is obviously the dynamic factor, the spirit moving the whole, which is the chief concern of education. The child at first is not capable of the highest. First comes physical constraint, which ought gradually to give place to the nobler forms of compulsion, issuing finally, if he be capable of it, in self-mastery based on intelligence, sympathy, and love. How the change can be effected will be described in the chapters that follow.

## CHAPTER TWO

### Education and Discipline

I T is now possible to give a definition of education. In its widest sense education is the
influence which, consciously or unconsciously,
society as a whole exercises over the development
and conduct of its individual members. In a
narrower sense it is the influence exercised by
one particular society, the school, over the development of the young, in order to prepare them
for their adult life.

So far all are agreed. Differences of opinion,
however, at once appear when the questions are
raised: what direction should this development
take? For what kind of life should the young be
prepared, and what should be the means employed? In other words, there are different views
about the Aims and Methods of schooling.

Roughly speaking, we may say that the aim
of education is fixed by public opinion, while the
methods are determined by schoolmasters themselves. Public opinion may choose well or ill; it
may, or it may not, be influenced or modified by
discussion and argument. But ultimately the
educational ideal, like all other ideals, is appre-
hended intuitively. If public opinion demand

vocational education, vocational education it will have. It cannot be reasoned out of its conviction. Of course time brings with it changes; indeed educational ideals vary from generation to generation, being determined by the *summum bonum* of the age. But as these changes are brought about by the gradual growth of the social conscience, it is perhaps of little use to discuss what the educational ideal ought to be, except in the broadest outlines.

When, however, the ultimate end is given, scientific discussion combined with careful experiment can ascertain the best means of reaching that end. My own experience has led me to the firm belief that the aim, whatever it may be, is best achieved by creating, through enlightened discipline, a feeling of obligation towards it that may be summed up in the two words "I must."

This subordinate aim, as it may be called, is really a reverence for law. There is no degradation in requiring children to cultivate it, as not even the greatest genius can afford to despise it. But of late there has grown up the idea that reverence is only another name for superstitious yielding to authority, and that the child mind learns best if it does not trouble overmuch about the laws underlying a subject. On the one hand we have the Heuristic Method, which aims at freeing the learner from the trammels of authority and placing him in such a position that he can discover truth for himself; on the other we have, in language-teaching, the relegation of grammar to a very subordinate position indeed. Now experience shows clearly the impracticable nature of both these points of view; but even were it possible to carry out moderately success-ful teaching on the lines indicated, the final re-sults would be deplorable. Disrespect for the laws of language obeyed by our great writers, and disregard of the scientific work accomplished by the pioneers in research, is not a good spirit for youth to learn in. After all, the young are immature learners; they are the heirs of a goodly heritage, and it is wrong to teach them to despise it.

The truth is that the pendulum has swung too far from the old view that blind respect for one's elders should govern the whole course of edu-cation. Admittedly, respect should not be blind, and its object should not be mere age. But these truths have been perverted into a blind worship of everything new, however lawless, however dubious the novelty may be. Such views are but the natural result of the revolution in thought which has taken place during the last fifty years or so—the triumph of youth over age. Transferred to the sphere of education this eman-cipation of youth has produced an over-estimate of the powers of childhood, which over-estimate in its turn has resulted in a cocksureness and

conceit that seriously endanger the future success
and happiness of those in our schools.

I do not imply or suggest that modern ten-
dencies in schooling are entirely erroneous. They
may be summed up in the precept, "Look at all
things from the standpoint of the child." This
precept is based upon the profound psychological
truth that child mentality is a very different thing
from adult mentality, so that failure is the inevitable result of leaving the former out of account. But this is a very different thing from
the conclusion that child mentality is complete
and perfect, and that it is spoilt by interference.
The teacher must understand the child mind,
but to say this is not to imply that he should be
content with it. His duty, in fact, is to guide the
child mind in its development, so that this is
normal and gradual, without any sudden breaks
or unprepared leaps into an over-strange environment. Mental growth, like physical growth,
ought to be as even and as regular as nature
permits. To be a fitting guide for immature
learners the teacher must live a sort of double
mental life; he must be able to think and feel as
a child, and yet at the same time to see the
imperfections of child thought, and to lead
it to something more mature and more complete.

But modern extremists are not content with
this. Unconsciously they act as though the first

rule of education was to destroy the past, and as far as possible to place the child on the first rung of the ladder of progress, leaving him to climb upwards as best he may. Of course this is not what they profess to do, nor, happily, is it what they actually accomplish; but their efforts tend in that direction, and their pupils' minds in consequence receive a wrong bent, or at best become purposeless and chaotic.

The old maxim of "do as you are told" was not so much wrong as incomplete. If the teacher goes no further, he becomes a tyrant and his charges become slaves. But if obedience be re-inforced, at first by trust and afterwards by a gradually increasing understanding of its necessity, if submission to a personality develop into intelligent submission to law, then the maxim does not fall far short of the truth.

A great deal has been written about encouraging originality and initiative in children. Much exaggeration occurs in these writings of the amount and quality of the originality which children are capable of showing. If, however, we exclude cases of rare genius, originality is of little value, and has a very limited scope, unless habit and discipline have impressed upon the student much of what has already been accomplished by his predecessors, and impressed it so thoroughly that its use is effortless and spontaneous. We see the truth of this in all forms of activity. Medical research cannot successfully be carried out by a man whose energies are distracted by efforts to remember half-learned pathology. The musical composer must know his harmony and counter-point so well that he can apply them uncon-sciously. Even unoriginal work needs an auto-matic foundation; the accountant must be a machine at figures. All the higher activities that need the conscious working of the mind require a foundation of spontaneous obedience to law, and this obedience can be secured only by dis-cipline and all that discipline implies. It is not necessary that the laws should be learnt in any particular way, though inductive reasoning comes more naturally to children, but learnt they must be, and that thoroughly. Surely it is not un-reasonable to urge that the function of schooling is to develop this automatic obedience to law, so that in the University, or in the greater school of Life, the necessary machinery for freer and nobler action may be as complete as possible. That the obedience should be enlightened, united, that is, with an intelligent and willing co-opera-tion, follows at once from what has been said about the nature of the best discipline. Such I take to be the character of education in schools, a character always essential, whatever may be the ulterior object which it is desired by education to achieve. In other words, schooling has a general method independent of the curriculum, and the immediate purpose of it is to inculcate habits and to give inspiration.

Needless to say, all institutions exercise some educational influence upon their members, and the school has by no means been always the most powerful and efficient of them. The home, exerting its influence during the most impressionable years of life, has been either a strong ally or a dangerous enemy of the school. We should note in passing that if the rule of "do as you please" were followed during the first seven years of life, few children would survive, and these few would be quite unfit to take part in any sort of school life. In mediaeval times the Church was the most important educational society, and gradually lost this character as church discipline declined. Ancient Greece and Rome found in the State their most powerful means of education, and Greek literature affords clear evidence that thinkers realised the essential parts played by obedience, sacrifice, and love in the rearing of citizens. From the multitude of passages that will at once suggest themselves to scholars I must be content with two; but these are so plain in their meaning that comment upon them would be superfluous.

The first is from Plato's *Crito*. Socrates, in support of his refusal to escape from prison, appeals to the Laws of Athens, which are supposed to address him thus[1]:

[1] *Crito* 51 A foll.

Are you too clever to realise that fatherland is something more precious than father and mother and all one's ancestors, grander and more sacred, held in greater honour both by gods and by men of intelligence? That duty requires a man to worship the fatherland, to submit to it more, and to flatter it more, when it is angry, than his father when he is angry? That he must either persuade the fatherland otherwise, or do whatsoever it commands, suffering quietly punishment, if it be ordered, whether stripes or bonds; and if it lead him to wounds or death in war, to go to war? That right demands this, and that a man must not yield or retreat or leave his post? That in war, in the law-courts, and everywhere, he must do what the State, his fatherland, orders, or else persuade it what right really is; and that, though it is impious to use force against mother or father, it is much more impious to use it against the fatherland?...If our words are true, your present attempt is a wrong to us. For we Laws begat you, reared you, educated you, and gave you a share in all the fair things we could.

The second passage is from Pericles' funeral speech over some Athenians who laid down their lives early in the Peloponnesian War[1]:

So died these men as became Athenians. You, their survivors, must determine to have as unfaltering a resolution in the field, though you may pray that it may have a happier issue. And not contented with ideas derived from words of the advantages which are bound up with the defence of your country, though these would furnish a valuable text to a speaker even before an audience so alive to them as the present, you must yourselves realise the power of Athens, and feed your eyes upon her from day to day, till love of her fills your

[1] Thucydides ii. 43 (Crawley's translation).

hearts; and then when all her greatness shall break upon you, you must reflect that it was by courage, sense of duty, and a keen feeling of honour in action that men were enabled to win all this, and that no personal failure in an enterprise could make them consent to deprive their country of their valour, but they laid it at her feet as the most glorious contribution they could offer.

Obedience to the State and love of the State—these were the foundation of Athenian greatness. Whether Athens was worthy of the obedience and the love is another matter, and does not detract from the sufficiency of a discipline based upon them to achieve a great purpose.

The City-state educated well because every citizen took an active part in the government of it. Action, practice, habituation—without these the loftiest purposes are fruitless. With the delegation of the functions of government to others, the State no longer educated effectively. At the present day we have almost ceased to associate the State with education, except in so far as the State controls the schools; it is now not a school itself, as it was in the best days of Athens[1], when the State was to the citizen what the school is now to the child.

The present condition of affairs was no doubt inevitable, and may, or may not, be for the ultimate good of the community. But the limitation

[1] Pericles called Athens "the school of Greece" (Thucydides II. 41).

of education to schooling has been disastrous to
the progress of educational science. Schooling is
but the beginning of a process which lasts as long
as the individual can be said to develop; as long,
that is, as new habits can be formed or old habits
modified. The laws of such a life-long process
are not clearly understood while our gaze is never
taken off the first period of it, however important that period may be.

## CHAPTER THREE

## The Control of Education; Theory and Practice

OF all the forces controlling the work of a school the strongest is public opinion. This exerts itself in various ways. Wherever public money, whether from the Board of Education or from local bodies, is expended by the governing body of a school, these organised embodiments of public opinion fix within limits both the content of the curriculum and the types of headmaster and assistant masters to whom its practical working is entrusted. Directly, the power of public bodies is not great, as they leave most technical matters to the headmaster; but indirectly it is supreme, as they can withhold their grants if their wishes are not carried out.

A few schools are independent of public grants. In some cases they are endowed, but none can afford to disregard the wishes of the select public whose sons fill the class-rooms.

Public opinion, of course, does not speak with one voice. Some parents require, or desire, one kind of education for their children; other parents have other views. Hence a variety among schools, secondary and technical education having many

types, primary education[1] being more stereotyped.

Public opinion expresses itself partly in the regulations of examining bodies. Originally framed
by University teachers and by educationists,
these regulations are rapidly being modified by
the force of public opinion and particularly by
the influence of the Board of Education. This
body, which in certain cases pays the examination fee, now claims to have a voice in determining
what the examination shall be and in what way
it shall be conducted. Examinations are becoming more and more universal, and in consequence more and more elastic.

Examinations are nowadays affected by the
criticism of school teachers, who after all are a
section of the public speaking with expert
knowledge.

Most schools, at least most secondary schools,
are greatly influenced by the wishes of parents.
The extent of this influence varies with the personal character of the headmaster, to a less degree
with that of the assistant masters. A parent
certainly ought not to be allowed to dictate, but
legitimate requests should receive respectful attention. If dissatisfied, a parent can usually

[1] The schools are mostly of one type, but in the higher
standards of a school some elasticity of curriculum is possible.
So in most secondary schools a choice is allowed between
French and German.

remove his child and send him to another school more in sympathy with his views[1]. While undue influence is obviously bad, it is equally obvious that harmonious co-operation between parents and schools is all for the good of education.

A third factor is the teacher, both head and assistant. Certain conditions exist within which the teacher must work. He must satisfy educational authorities; he must do his best to please parents; he must produce a certain result to be tested by certain examinations. But he is allowed a practically free choice of methods, and his is the great privilege of doing much more than is actually required of him. He is expected to impart a minimum of instruction and to form habits of discipline; but when this is achieved, or rather while it is being achieved, he may, if he wish, educate boys in the true sense of the term, making them "fit to serve God in Church and State."

Another factor, perhaps the last of the important factors, is boy-nature. This cannot be changed by education; it can only be moulded and trained. Boys are becoming more and more conscious of the fact that the future is theirs, and that society is not static. They want to be pre-

[1] A parent has little influence over the working of a primary school. When all due account has been taken of the ignorance of the parent and of the non-payment of fees, this influence falls far short of the ideal. A change for the better will be slow, but is bound to come in time.

pared, not for the world as it is, but for the world as it may be a generation hence. In brief, boy-nature, though malleable, is in its essence un-alterable. There is a fixity in it which no other factor in education, and no combination of fac-tors, can possibly change. A recognition of this truth accounts for most of the educational re-forms of the last generation.

In discussing those influences which deter-mine educational practice stress has been laid upon "what is" rather than upon "what ought to be." Although every teacher should have his ideals, and strive to realise them as far as in him lies, yet he must never forget that he is not a free-lance. He has no right to ignore the views of others, because upon all lies the responsibility of deciding what the future will be. He is not omniscient, and it is something of an imperti-nence for him to dictate to parents what ideals they ought to have for their children. Even though he happens to be right and all others wrong, yet to prove that this is so cannot be demonstrated by logic. The final arbiter in all educational problems is experience, from which the truth emerges only by slow and painful degrees.

In one respect the authority of the teacher is supreme. When his task has been assigned, he should be allowed a free hand in carrying it out. The aim is given him by society (though he may persuade society to modify it) but the method is his own. He is the master of the means, but only in part the framer of the end.

The remarks I have just made illustrate what is perhaps the most striking truth of educational practice. A teacher's work is a mass of compromises. There are few, if any, principles which can be carried fully and consistently to their logical conclusions. Teaching is an art which demands the harmonising of factors often in part contradictory or inconsistent. The "whole-hogger" usually has an unpleasant time, and probably does much more harm than good. The teacher has to learn the old truth that the half is better than the whole, to refuse to be a die-hard, and to aim always at the happy mean. Reforms in education should be introduced gradually, cautiously, tentatively, with an ever-watchful readiness to retreat when danger threatens. A method, or an ideal, may be good, yet the teacher may find by bitter experience that he is not equal to it. When he realises this he should retire and take a safe course, not in despair, not in disgust, but with the conviction that, while for the present he must be content with a second best, yet continued effort and clearer thinking may enable him sooner or later to travel along the better way and to win the nobler prize.

Teaching is an art, and, like other arts, is dependent upon sciences for its principles and rules.

It may be objected that many excellent teachers have made no special study of these sciences without thereby losing efficiency. But this criticism ignores the truth that every educated man intuitively picks up a few of the main laws of ethics, psychology, and logic, and applies them subconsciously. Successful teaching is inevitably based upon these laws, and the only debatable question is the extent to which conscious and systematic knowledge is necessary or useful. It may be admitted at once that the mechanical application of a psychological principle is almost certain to do more harm than good. The teacher will be confused by his attention being withdrawn from his work and directed towards a different although allied subject. A cyclist must not while cycling think about the laws of equilibrium, nor should an organist while playing direct his thoughts to the principles of harmony and counterpoint. In both cases success requires spontaneous obedience to rules learnt beforehand. Yet there is another side to the question. The cyclist may manage fairly well by mere "knack" alone, but he will be a safer rider if he learns how skidding is caused. The organist too can reproduce the works of others without knowing anything of the theory of music; but originality is impossible unless scientific knowledge has been learnt, remembered, and digested so thoroughly that its application is automatic and independent of the will. So it is with teaching. Knowledge of theory is of no avail unless it is too thoroughly assimilated to be an obtrusive hindrance. It must be, not an ingredient of the teacher's work, but as it were a chemical component, or, to change the metaphor, the spirit animating the whole body.

In one respect the teacher is at a great disadvantage as compared with other artists. The sciences upon which his work depends have not the stability possessed by chemistry, biology, or physics. Logic indeed has fixed and reliable laws in which the teacher may place his trust, but ethics and psychology are anything but "exact" sciences. Psychology seems to the outside observer to change its character from year to year, while moral ideals, the subject-matter of ethics, often vary in a most perplexing manner. How can a teacher reasonably adopt with confidence a psychological "law" which flatly contradicts its predecessor of ten years ago?

So kaleidoscopic an uncertainty causes many a teacher to distrust all theory and to belittle or despise the training of which theory forms an important, in fact an essential, element.

Yet the answer to these perplexing doubts is ready to hand. Education should avoid altogether those "laws" which are in reality nothing but dubious and tentative hypotheses, or at any rate use them sparingly and cautiously in well-

guarded experiments. There are enough cer-
tainties, or at least high probabilities, to form a
firm foundation for education, even though one
might wish that this foundation were a little
wider. "Keep to the safe path" is a sound rule
to follow in all educational matters, partly and
perhaps chiefly because the material with which
the teacher works is too precious to endanger it
needlessly. Experiments should be carefully controlled and never thoughtlessly entered upon.
It is a sad sight to see the light-hearted way in
which some teachers are attracted by a fad and
rigidly apply it, regardless of consequences. Often
only their energy and enthusiasm prevent a
tragedy in the intellectual life of their pupils.
Herein public examinations, a much criticised
institution, often do good work by dragging the
visionary from the clouds to earth. Not one
teacher in a thousand has the insight, force of
character, and technical skill to be a pioneer and
perhaps a martyr.

The question is often debated whether there
is a science of education, separate from those
sciences which education uses as auxiliaries. In
other words, is there a mass of educational
material sufficient to produce generalisations,
numerous and capable of verification, which can
be reduced to a systematic whole? Are there
enough sequences of phenomena which reduce
themselves to hypotheses, verifiable by experi-

ment, and so changing first to theories and then to laws? In time such a science will doubtless exist, but it can hardly be said to exist as yet. Observations indeed have been made and experiments carried out, but they have been sporadic and unorganised. The results have never been thoroughly examined, and many fruitful lines of inquiry have never been worked at all. I will give but one example. Every schoolmaster knows that a boy's capacities of work and of attention vary with the time of day. It would be of great value to education if it could be discovered by experiment and tabulation of results what subjects are best suited to the various school hours at the different ages of school life. So far as I am aware, however, no such experiments have ever been attempted, at any rate on an adequate scale.

The science of education, when in being, will not be an exact science. It will consist of generalisations which are usually true while allowing numerous exceptions. The human material with which teachers work shows infinite variety, and teachers themselves are not of one type. Once more the great truth must be emphasised that rigidity is impossible in education, and teaching cannot be stereotyped. The teacher must be so sensitive to his environment that he can adapt himself to changed conditions at a moment's notice and be all things to all boys.

## CHAPTER FOUR

## The Curriculum, or What we Teach

THERE are certain fundamental principles which experience and thoughtful study have laid down for the framing of a school curriculum. Two of them are primary; the others are of the nature of corollaries.

The two primary principles[1] emphasise the claims of utility and of culture, "utility" being used in its narrow sense and "culture" in its widest. The assumptions are made that a boy must be prepared to earn his living, and that he will be not only a wage-earner but also a man and a citizen. It follows that the curriculum will be wide, for culture demands that no important department of knowledge should be wholly neg-

[1] A first principle is an ultimate rule which must be either rejected or accepted without discussion. If it be disputed, it must be carried for decision to a higher court. If, for instance, an opponent should dispute the principle that the curriculum ought to be utilitarian, the question can be decided only by leaving the narrower sphere of the curriculum and referring to the definition of school education in general. Should this definition also be disputed, education must give place to ethics, and some agreement be reached as to what is the good for man. As soon as the opponents are agreed, the process must be reversed, and they must work downwards until the original principle is confirmed or rejected.

lected. It is impossible to include every natural science, yet one or other ought to be an integral part of every school course. On the other hand, should the curriculum be too general, nothing can be learned thoroughly, as there is no time for concentration. Both utility and culture require a certain degree of specialisation. One's life-work usually centres in a limited group of studies and activities, and a boy who never learns at least one thing fully and well will never know what excellence really is and how great is his own ignorance. Accordingly, there must be here, as nearly everywhere in education, a compromise between factors which cannot be completely harmonised. The final result may not be ideal, but it should be the best that conditions permit.

There are a few subjects, such as reading, which every school must teach; but many varieties of curriculum are the necessary result of adapting it to the district in which the school is, to the probable careers of the boys, and to the usual age for leaving school. Indeed, one might almost say, *quot pueri, tot curricula.*

The line of division between "useful" and "cultural" subjects is not a rigid one. Some of the best work done by modern educationists has been in the direction of getting the greatest amount of true culture out of vocational training. To take an obvious instance. Agriculture was once a narrow, technical subject; it is now one

of the finest examples of vocational work connected at all points with the sciences, the arts,
and life generally. Nevertheless, there are certain refinements which do not usually fall within
the range of vocational training and yet are
essential components of a liberal education.
Music, painting, and literature come within this
class, and experience shows that it is not wise to
leave them too much to chance. Wherever a
spark of love for them exists it should receive
every possible encouragement. They are inex-
pensive recreations, truly restful, doubly needed
in an impoverished age of feverish activities.

In at least one other respect the curriculum of
to-day is an improvement on that of a generation
ago. Gradually but surely education is becoming
less bookish. Boys are set to make things rather
than to read about them. Experiments, handi-
crafts, the manufacture of useful articles, gar-
dening and various forms of nature-study—all
these pursuits rejoice the heart of middle-aged
men, who look back upon school-days spent in
studying books and in writing, with nothing, or
next to nothing, to vary the tedium that came
from sitting still hour after hour in the same
room.

The modern educational motto, "Look at
things from the point of view of the child," has
in truth been responsible for much happy progress. It seems therefore churlish and ungrateful

to criticise it harshly. But the criticism is directed not so much against the motto as against its over-enthusiastic followers. One of the worst mistakes in modern education is the tendency to emasculate a subject, or even to omit it altogether, in order to eliminate everything that is irksome. If a subject really be too difficult for boys it ought not to be taught at all until they have developed enough to profit by the study. If it be uninteresting and unnecessary as well, it ought to be entirely excluded from the curriculum. If it be necessary and not above their powers, it should be attacked bravely, and not ruined by the omission of the parts that boys happen not to like. Boys are sure to take the line of least resistance; they may be good judges of what interests them at the present, but they do not know what will interest them in a few years' time.

Of course some stimulus, some incentive, is a necessity. When the ultimate end of a course of study is within the comprehension of a boy it should be explained to him; when he cannot appreciate it, he should take it on trust from a master in whom he has complete confidence. But to make the likes and dislikes of immature minds the test of what should, or should not, occupy school life saps the moral fibre and is the worst possible preparation for life in the world.

It may be urged that childhood ought not to be occupied with unpleasant tasks, which will

bear fruit only later on; that it may be cut short
by premature death, and should therefore be regarded not merely as a period of preparation for
the future, but as an end in itself. Nobody denies
this. No modern school will fail to teach much
of its serious work by means of spontaneous
play; the tendency is all in the direction of utili-
sing the play-instinct to the full. But it is a mistake to include nothing in the curriculum that
cannot be dealt with as play. "Drudgery for
drudgery's sake" is a long-discarded doctrine;
but to reduce all work to play is to misunderstand
boy-nature and to rob childhood of one of its
highest and keenest joys. Boys, at any rate boys
of twelve or thirteen, have a dim consciousness
that life is composed of other things besides play.
They are just beginning to realise that some tasks
are necessary, yet bring little pleasure except that
of successful accomplishment. But their way-
ward impulses are not yet under control, and
they respect, admire, and even love a masterful
man who can lend them his strength until they
can govern themselves. The necessary stimulus
is thus in the first place the master's personality.

Many writers eloquently plead that effort without interest is like slave-labour—unprofitable,
exhausting, and demoralising. But the interest
need not be the partial interest of the moment.
A far more important, though more remote, interest is a truly successful life. When boys begin

to appreciate the truth that more immediately attractive pursuits compete with this ulterior purpose they are, more than at any other time, in need of a leader who will make them work for him until they have grown strong enough to work for an ideal.

NOTE. The reader is asked to bear in mind that in this chapter I refer to a boy's liking for a subject and not to his ability to study it successfully. If a boy has no power to progress in a subject, that is a very good reason for allowing him if possible to drop it.

## CHAPTER FIVE

## *How we Learn*

Psychologists have not yet determined exactly what the laws of learning are, but there are a few propositions which not only have been accepted by the experts but also are sanctioned by general experience.

One is that new material cannot be properly assimilated until the learner's mind is prepared to receive it. We interpret fresh impressions in the light of past experience, and if this past experience be insufficient, our interpretation, though possibly sound logically, will be wrong in the sense that it will not correspond with reality. The little slum child who, having never seen the plant before, called a fern "a pot of green feathers," possessed a brain which functioned correctly, but was unequipped with the knowledge necessary to understand the object-lesson which the schoolmistress was proposing to give her. This example illustrates clearly the danger involved in ill-regulated teaching. The mistake is obvious when pointed out, yet it is surprising how often it is made even by experienced teachers. The only way to meet the danger is for the teacher to satisfy himself by repeated questioning that each fresh stage is understood before the next is attempted. This precaution is often irksome to pupils, and the teacher has need of great powers of control if it is to be successfully carried out.

Knowledge, then, grows through the learner's interpreting aright new experiences and amalgamating them properly with past experiences; skill, on the other hand, grows through the formation of correct habits. The sciences are composed chiefly of knowledge, the arts chiefly of skill, but every subject really comprises both. Theory and practice must ever go together, though theory sometimes predominates, as in mathematics, while practice predominates in subjects like music and painting. In the case of language-learning expert opinion is divided. Some teachers rely on practice, reducing theory to a minimum; others hold that a considerable amount of theory is usually necessary. As all studies, being to some extent arts, require practice, the second principle of learning may be summed up in the proposition that progress depends upon the formation of good and lasting habits.

Of these habits the most fundamental is that of doing one's best, no matter what the proposed task may be. A boy can acquire at school no better possession for his life in the world than the determination to do as well as possible whatever his hand and brain find to do. On the other hand his worst handicap is the habit of resting content with work that falls short of the degree of excellence a greater effort could have achieved. Self-respect suffers when one constantly realises that a poor result is due to carelessness or to laziness, until the conscience is so dulled that the worker acquiesces in anything. Moreover, although we often find persons conscientious in one respect and unconscientious in others, slackness is of all qualities the most liable to be transferred from one form of activity to another.

The third principle of learning is that the learner needs a stimulus. The emotions play a large part in the acquisition of knowledge and skill, particularly when the learner is young and the habit of learning has not become spontaneous and automatic. Motives, however, are nearly always mixed, and a warning is necessary that in any particular case more than one stimulus is probably operating. But of the components which make up a given impulse to learn, one usually is dominant and modifies all the others, giving them a distinctive characteristic or colour.

Some incentives to learn are due to the pleasure derived from the subject itself, which, should desire follow, is then said to have an interest for us. Interest is perhaps the most powerful incentive to learn, and a wise teacher will attach great importance to it. When it exists, the battle is half won, and no healthy interest should be allowed to die of atrophy, as the complexity of modern life requires that a man should give a sympathetic attention to matters unheard-of a generation ago.

When we are interested in a thing, we consider that it has value and is worth our time and attention.

Sometimes an interest is momentary, that is, the interesting object claims our attention as being the most attractive thing in our immediate environment. The prisoner in his cell is deeply interested in many things which, in other circumstances, would pass unnoticed—a flower, a mouse, or even an insect. A game of patience or an old newspaper is interesting when we have "nothing better to do." So too in the class-room, if more attractive occupations are rendered impossible, interest in the lesson, while not necessarily assured—a boy may take refuge in his own thoughts—is at any rate greatly stimulated.

Permanent interests are occasionally the outcome of passing interests, but they usually spring from individual tastes and capacities. Often in the young they exist as mere potentialities, and one of the functions of the educator is to discover such potentialities and to develop them. Within limits a man ought to be interested in as many things as possible. The qualifying phrase "within limits" is added because a many-sided person may easily dissipate his energies and consequently make a success of nothing.

The weakness of interests as a stimulus to learning lies in their narrow and partial nature. They may be sufficient for the teacher, but they are not enough for the educator. They are an uncertain foundation upon which to build a character and a life. Concentration upon one's pet subject may be an essential condition for complete success in that subject, and a medical man, for example, is not worth his salt if he does not find his profession of absorbing interest. But success can be bought at too high a price. It may involve neglect òf duties. It may mean a one-sidedness justifiable only by the rarest genius. In the great majority of cases a compromise has to be effected between interests and obligations, between duty to oneself and duty to one's neighbour.

There are things which appeal to us indirectly and not directly. We can be interested in work, not for its own sake, but because it is a means to a desired end. A boy interested in engineering will cheerfully undertake any task which he realises will make him a better engineer. Sometimes, however, the ultimate end of a necessary course of study is beyond the comprehension of the young mind. The stimulus then is of necessity artificial. The desire to please parents and teachers, to do honour to one's school, to compete honourably with one's fellows—all these things are useful stimulants if used at the right

time and in moderation. The instinct of pugna-
city, generally directed against competitors, may
also be directed against the work itself. That
difficulties exist only to be overcome should be
the motto of every school. The scholar should
be encouraged to compete, not so much with his
class-mates as with himself. The system, adopted
in some schools, of representing a boy's efforts
by a weekly percentage instead of by a place in
an order of merit, enables him to compare his
past self with his present self. This pugnacious
attitude towards difficulties is largely a matter of
habit and of living contact with a strong tradition.

The charge is often brought against modern
education that it turns bright material into list-
less and lazy youths, with no learning and no
wish to learn. It is suggested that the cause is
the uninteresting nature of the teaching. The
truth, however, is that these boys are often sated
and jaded. Their whims have been humoured
until gratification is robbed of its charm. The
way has been made too easy, the work too
pleasant. They have not learnt the great lesson
that the attainment of our highest good demands
self-sacrifice. Either they have no ideals or they
will not pay the price of their realisation.

Nobody is free always to do as he pleases.
Checks and restraints are ever hampering or
controlling our actions; to ignore these is folly

and to struggle against them is useless. An ideal involves the cheerful performance of many tasks not directly connected with that ideal. Our individuality and originality can be sanely developed only when we are willing and able to go through the daily round efficiently and without irritation. Drudgery should be reduced to a minimum, but it must never be shirked. It must be transformed by love into loyal service to our most cherished purpose.

## CHAPTER SIX

## Teaching

TEACHING is but a part of education. Education is the influence of society upon human growth; a teacher is merely a guide to learning. The sphere of education is the whole development of an individual; the sphere of teaching is the individual's mastery of a given subject or subjects. We teach French, mathematics, or natural science; we educate children.

Again, although teaching and learning are correlative, they are not exactly so. Children are always learning, whether they are being taught or not. They are always assimilating new material, and forming new habits, physical, moral, and intellectual. Teaching is but the sum total of the master's efforts to guide this learning, and a child learns far more than he is ever taught.

Incidentally we must notice that the teacher's responsibility is as great as that of the educator who fixes the curriculum. His duty is to foster those habits which will be most useful, not at the moment, but a generation ahead. He must effect the happiest possible compromise between conservatism and radicalism. He must strive after that stability which comes only from fixed habits, while leaving unimpaired the adaptability necessary to meet new difficulties and to solve new problems. The heritage of the past must be preserved without sacrificing the hope of the future. Good teaching should foster the habit of originality. Discipline, indeed, need not stifle either originality or initiative. It may, in fact, develop them, for self-trained originality usually lacks thoroughness, and untrained originality leads to nowhere.

Some authorities attach so much importance to originality, in the wider sense of the term, that they maintain that the individual really knows only that which he has taught himself. As it stands, the assertion is misleading, but it expresses imperfectly the basic principle of all true teaching, that success varies with the active co-operation between learner and teacher. Progress depends primarily upon the will to learn; and it is only when the teacher has made the learners ready and willing to learn from him that his knowledge and capacity are of the slightest use.

To secure the good-will of his scholars is every teacher's duty. It is the foundation without which a sound superstructure is impossible. His task is not so much to make a subject interesting as to make boys interested in a subject. Unfortunately there is no golden rule by the help of which we can win over the young to co-operate with us. The secret cannot be learnt by any rule of thumb; it is more a matter of the heart than of the head. Sympathy with children and a selfless desire to help them are the most essential characteristics of a successful teacher; but the best definition of a schoolmaster would be a modification of Cato's definition of an orator. He is *vir bonus docendi peritus*, "a good man, practised in teaching." The technique of the art, important as it is, is but secondary; the primary thing is human excellence, every kind of which adds greatly to a schoolmaster's value, provided that there exists the essential foundation of intelligent sympathy with children.

Perhaps "devotion" would be a better expression by which to denote this basic quality of good teaching. There is a singleness of purpose, a concentration of effort, in the work of the best schoolmasters which is but feebly indicated, if indicated at all, in "selfless sympathy." The objection to the term "devotion" is that it does not suggest intelligence; it is, in fact, often found in stupid persons. Possibly the best way to express the quality would be by the cumbrous phrase "intelligent and sympathetic devotion to the well-being of the young[1]."

[1] The reader should notice that I am speaking of the teacher rather than of the educator. The basic quality for an educator is intelligent leadership, the power to persuade the young to form good habits. As nobody can be a good teacher without being a good educator, leadership is pre-supposed in our definition of the ideal schoolmaster.

However difficult it may be to find the best words to describe the most essential characteristic of a good teacher, the thing itself is easily recognised. Presence at a very few lessons is enough to tell an experienced observer whether a man has in him the right spirit to become a successful teacher. Should this spirit be present, the best advice to be given to a young teacher is that he should think for himself and learn to solve his own problems, while paying due attention to the experience gained by his predecessors. Loving meditation on the difficulties of his work will go very far towards solving them.

The co-operation of teacher and taught can be considered from another standpoint. How is the teacher to capture and to keep the attention of his pupils? Attention, or the concentration of one's mind on a given object, may be secured by the teacher in various ways, of which three must be briefly examined.

Let us picture to ourselves once more the young master face to face with his class. He is ready to impart knowledge, and he fondly believes that the boys are equally ready to receive it. As a matter of fact, out of a class of thirty, perhaps five will be eager to learn[1], five will be

---

[1] In any class there may be a case of the over-conscientious boy, who is *too* eager to learn, and so may later on develop serious nerve trouble. Happily such cases are rare.

keen not to learn, and twenty will be indifferent.
If our tiro could only be inside his boys' minds,
one by one, he would certainly have many shocks
of surprise, and probably would receive the most
valuable lesson in teaching that he is ever likely
to enjoy. Boys' minds differ very much with
their age and previous up-bringing, but they all
are both lively and fickle, jumping lightly from
one thing to another at the bidding of the slightest
stimulus or even of mere caprice. This quality
is of great use in that it is the foundation of that
flexibility which insures progress and encourages
initiative. But by itself it can lead only to chaos.
Before real improvement can take place this
flexibility must be controlled.

As our young master comes into his form-
room for the first time he will certainly arouse
the interest of his boys. One will silently criticise his manner or dress; another will be estimating his athletic powers; nearly all will be
sub-consciously speculating what sort of a disciplinarian he is likely to prove. Now the
master's duty is to direct the boys' attention from
these and similar subjects to the lesson of the
hour. They must be made to realise that it
has real claims upon them. They must learn to
resist distractions, however attractive, and to
concentrate their powers of thought on the
matter in hand. In short, the master has not
only to keep order but also to retain attention.

There are three ways of doing this. The first is that of the bully with a thick stick. There are times that call for vigorous methods backed up by corporal punishment; the mistake of the bully is to appeal to these on the slightest provocation. He places fear, and that the crudest form of fear, in the foreground. He makes his first resource that which should be the last. Consequently he gets results, but not the best results; for an atmosphere pervaded by fear is not conducive to healthy mental growth. Morally, moreover, the bully does harm by visiting mere inattention with penalties which ought to be reserved for serious offences.

The second way of securing attention is that favoured by most extremists among modern writers on education. It is generally known as arousing interest. The master eliminates as far as possible the more laborious and less interesting parts of the subject, and concentrates on those for which the boys seem to have a liking. He hopes, indeed, that in time these disagreeable parts will be faced and mastered, but he postpones the evil day.

This view too is sound in so far as it takes into account the psychology of the child-mind in determining method, but it is a serious mistake to allow the vagaries of that mind to become the determining factor in the situation. It is right to make work interesting, but it is wrong to allow boys to decide entirely what they are interested in. There are many things that boys can do well, and with a happy, healthy interest, which are nowadays often rejected as unsuitable. The secret of success lies in the personality of the teacher and the way in which he attacks the problems of teaching.

The right way to secure and retain the attention of a class is, while never setting them a task above their powers, to convince them that the work is worth while. Possibly it may not be especially attractive in itself. If so, it is all the more important to impress upon the boys, not by preaching, but by the suggestive force of the teacher's attitude to it, that an extra effort is required. The atmosphere of the class-room should be one of strenuous endeavour. Successful achievement should be taken for granted by the teacher. If he be sympathetic and gifted with a sense of humour, giving help where help is needed while setting his face against "spoon-feeding," he will in time infect the class with his own spirit. When finally the boys feel the pleasurable thrill of successful accomplishment, another step will have been gained in the battle for self-mastery.

But even when the teacher has won the attention of his class, that is to say, has made them interested in their work, he has not necessarily secured their co-operation, although he has made definite progress in the right direction. Both interest and attention may be merely passive; an attentive and interested listener may learn little or nothing. Successful teaching implies that an active interest has been aroused, an interest which is not content with mere understanding but insists upon performance. Here again an honourable fear may accomplish much, while a natural taste for a subject is almost bound to lead to successful effort. But neither of these forms of stimulus is sufficient, although a little of the former is no bad thing, while it is impossible to have too much of the latter. What is needed as a foundation is a stimulus which will act even when fear is removed and interest has waned or died.

Is there such a stimulus? Surely it can be found in the habit of work based upon a sense of duty. In this there is a life-long possession which continues to act when other incentives fail, and yet can be re-inforced by such incentives to the utmost degree. To foster this habit is one of a schoolmaster's chief duties.

It is strange that schoolboy tradition has long been hostile to hard work. This hostility dates from the time master and boys were natural enemies, and has been kept alive by stupid methods of teaching and by the overloading of the curriculum with more subjects than a boy can adequately deal with. But, whatever its origin, it is one of the most serious obstacles to education, and the schoolmaster must do his utmost to remove it. By himself, perhaps, he can accomplish little, but his efforts should be part of a united struggle by the school authorities. A good school ought to have a tradition of earnest effort. Slacking at French or mathematics should be condemned by schoolboy ethics no less than slacking at football. The atmosphere of a school decides what each individual boy thinks, and the atmosphere is determined by the ideals and will-power of the educators[1] who control the school.

Fear as an incentive to effort has already been discussed, and though crude fear makes the learner a slave who hates his work, yet it may be sublimated into an honourable dread of falling short of one's best, and thus bringing disgrace upon oneself and probably unhappiness to one's parents. Shame, in fact, is a refined form of fear, and shame before others naturally develops into one of our highest emotions—shame before the ideal self.

Our discussion of motives has led us to the conclusion that the basic incentive for a schoolboy is the will to succeed, encouraged by a healthy school tradition and developed by habits of hard work. The joy of successful endeavour

[1] The word "educators" is used advisedly. All the authorities of the school, and the parents themselves, play a part. *Quod semper, quod ubique, quod ab omnibus,* describes education perfectly. An influence felt always and everywhere is the influence that truly educates.

is a natural result, which in its turn becomes a powerful stimulus and commonly creates and fosters, if it does not exist already, a lively and intelligent interest.

Successful teaching has yet another character-istic. The teacher must know his subject, love it, and be convinced of its value. The effect upon a class of such a teacher, if he has sympathy with boy-nature, is astonishing. He creates an atmosphere favourable to learning. Dormant interests manifest themselves, and the dullest intellects are sometimes inspired to successful achievement. The influence of suggestion, un-consciously exerted and unconsciously received, has full scope to act, and cannot fail to produce the most far-reaching results. Many a man owes his career to teaching of this type, and acknow-ledges his debt with both gratitude and affection.

One of the most insidious mistakes into which an otherwise good teacher can fall is that of making the task of learning too easy. It is the defect of a virtue, and herein lies its danger. While a teacher's duty is to make the path to knowledge plain and smooth, the error of excess is as fatal as that of defect. The road may be so clear that the scholar never learns how to learn; he gains knowledge at the cost of his self-reliance. The teacher has done for him work which he ought to have done for himself. In consequence a most important lesson is never mastered, that valuable possessions must be paid for by toil and labour. The teacher has paid the scholar's debt and led him to expect "ninepence for fourpence." Help ceases to be a virtue and becomes a vice when it makes a task easier than it need be for the learner to perform it with a reasonable expenditure of effort.

It is when the teacher has been unable to arouse the necessary stimulus that he is tempted to give too much help. Progress is slow, and he tries to drag his scholars along. He carries them not only when the road is too steep, but also when they are perfectly able to walk, or even to run, by themselves. Yet a boy's life at school has been wasted unless it has prepared him to deal intelligently and decisively with the situations that arise during the course of his later career, when the only staff he has to lean upon is himself.

Moreover, boys enjoy being made to work. Even the young can appreciate the truth that self-control, discipline, the habit of cheerfully overcoming difficulties, diligence, and self-reliance are more likely to bring success than the gratification of an interest or of a few interests. Perhaps the realisation is at first dim and imperfect, but the suggestive influence of parents and teachers can make the ideal of an active, useful, and healthy life clearer and brighter, until it becomes a permanent possession, a guide to conduct so long as life lasts.

## CHAPTER SEVEN

## Teachers and their Training

IF the conclusions reached in the last chapter are true, good teaching is no easy matter. To foster habits inspired by a strong life-purpose is not within the power of a nonentity. Preaching is of no use, as it makes prigs of the few and disgusted rebels of the many. *Disciplina* is the result of character acting upon character; it cannot be created by formula. Much scorn has been poured upon those who have been styled "teachers by the grace of God." Yet undoubtedly some men exercise a natural magnetic influence over boys. The mere presence of such a man produces an atmosphere of diligence and attention. The possession of this indefinable power is a great asset and vastly increases the efficacy of those characteristics which the good teacher ought to possess.

Whatever its real nature may be, and probably there are several kinds of it, the power to make boys work is indispensable. Education implies the formation of habits of a desired type, and habits can not be acquired except by repeated acts. If a teacher cannot succeed in effecting this process, he is useless. It is not enough to keep order and to keep attention; discipline, that is, ordered activity, must be maintained.

If this be so, how can teachers be prepared for their profession? There is a wide-spread opinion, especially common among headmasters, that the training of teachers is of no value, or even harmful. When all due allowance has been made for prejudice, some element of truth must be contained in a view so generally held by competent critics. Let us therefore examine briefly the curriculum adopted by our training colleges.

Students in training study in some detail the theory of education and do a certain amount of school practice under the supervision of their instructors. The idea underlying the course is that a teacher is less likely to fall into a groove if he learns the psychology of the child-mind and the efforts that have been made by great educators to adapt education to the laws of that psychology. It is expected that a broad-mindedness will result which afterwards will derive a maximum of benefit from the lessons of experience. The practical side of the training is supposed to eliminate the worst faults of technique before the schoolmaster takes up a post on the staff of a school. The result hoped for is, not an experienced teacher, but one prepared to learn his art quickly and intelligently.

Headmasters complain that a man who has gone through a training college is generally a weak disciplinarian, who is so much occupied with theoretical considerations of what he ought to do, or not to do, that he can neither keep order nor make his class work. They accordingly prefer a beginner to be untrained, and to have no preconceptions to confuse his mind and hamper his freedom. He will then fall more easily into the ways of the school, instead of trying to reform these ways by applying misunderstood, or half-understood, speculations of unpractical theorists.

One cannot help thinking that the usual course of training is too ambitious. It lasts less than a year, and in the space of a few months an attempt is made to study the principles and history of education, the outlines of psychology, logic, and ethics, with perhaps the special methods of teaching one or more subjects. Even the most able men can acquire no more than a smattering of so many topics in so short a time, and they have little or no opportunity of correlating theory with experience and practice. It is doubtful whether any benefit accrues to a beginner from a study of educational theory which cannot be put to the test of experience, while it is certain that much positive harm is done by vague knowledge and misconceptions. A better syllabus would be one combining the fundamental principles of educational theory with the best ways of applying them to actual practice. The worst result of the present system is that the science of education tends to be dissociated from the art of teaching. Where there should be interaction there is isolation. If the student could learn to combine the two sides of his work within a limited area, he would be enabled to carry over to his professional career a habit capable of being developed as his experience increased. Instead of casting aside his text-books when his period of training ends, he would be stimulated to continue his studies, especially now that excellent "summer schools" are organised by various associations and by the Board of Education.

Improvement of the curriculum, however, would not by itself produce the right type of trained teacher. The men who offer themselves for training are rarely the best material. Conscious of their weaknesses, some of them are trying to improve their qualifications. Many are attracted by the handsome grants paid by the Board of Education. If a man is accepted for training by a University and promises on the conclusion of his course to teach in State-aided schools, he receives from the Board about £200, spread over the four years during which he is reading for a degree and undergoing a course of training. These generous terms are intended to attract the most suitable men for the teaching profession, but they really amount to the endowment of mediocrity. The most promising teachers can get employment straight away without being trained; those who join the training department are usually either "weaklings," or poor men anxious to secure a University education even by undertaking to do work for which they are not naturally qualified. The intentions of the Board of Education are excellent, but the results are lamentable.

We are a people who spend money lavishly on education. The organisation of it is elaborate and expensive. The buildings erected during recent years are palatial and thoroughly equipped. The physical needs of children are attended to so well that some critics think that the young people of this generation are pampered and spoilt. The curriculum is a subject in which everybody is interested, and the faults of modern curricula are a popular subject of discussion in the daily press. But about the one thing needful there is general indifference. The choice of teachers is left to chance. It is not realised how uncommon are the qualities required for successful teaching, and how poor the result of education is unless schoolmasters possess them. In fact, teachers as a class are despised. The scholastic profession is popularly regarded as a refuge for those destitute of the forceful qualities necessary for success in walks of life leading to prosperity and distinction. The long holidays and comparatively short hours are grudgingly considered compensation for a career of obscurity and poverty.

This conception is radically wrong. The living factor in teaching is far more important than organisation and material equipment, possibly more important even than the curriculum. If one twentieth part of the money spent in organisation were intelligently applied in discovering the best candidates for the profession, and if one half the outlay on buildings were devoted to making that profession attractive, most of our educational difficulties would disappear in a generation. Energetic leaders, with the power to influence boys, could be found if we really wished to find them, and a very short training would fit them at least to commence as probationers.

One possible method of procedure may be given, merely as an example, in a little more detail. The authorities of Universities and of University Colleges might be allowed to choose, from undergraduates, candidates who apparently have the necessary qualities, and these, if willing, might be given on graduation a short trial of, say, three weeks in a school, and if they proved satisfactory they could be accepted on probation. After working for a year, or possibly two years, would come a period of training, to last for not less than two terms and not more than three, according to the degree of proficiency shown. Then the teacher might reasonably be considered fully qualified.

Difficulties in the way of adopting this plan will occur to all, but resolution and care could overcome them. Of one thing we can be certain. Suitable men would be glad enough to accept the scheme if the financial prospects were good. They would not be loth to devote part of their vacations, as University teachers do, to preparation for the next term's work, if such preparation were considered an integral part of the duties for which they were paid. Attendance at conferences and at summer schools, the study of educational theory, and the planning of experiments could become normal instead of exceptional. The only necessary conditions are the right type of men and remuneration high enough to attract them.

CHAPTER EIGHT

## The Technique of Teaching

TEACHING is an art, and like other arts has its own technique. A good technique contributes much towards the success of a teacher in obtaining from his pupils habitual excellence of performance. One of the most exasperating trials of a teacher is the uncertainty of a scholar's work. Sometimes little fault can be found with it. Then something is submitted which makes the master despair of success. Reliability is lacking; the class cannot be depended upon. Every stage of education is liable to show these lapses, from Standard I of the Primary School to honours students at the University.

The most common reason for this defect is faulty teaching technique. If a teacher finds repeatedly that he has overestimated the progress of his scholars, that their accuracy is apparently a matter of chance upon which no reliance can be placed, he may be sure that the necessary habits have not yet been formed, and fairly certain that he himself has violated the most fundamental principle of the art of teaching. He has been too active and his pupils have been too passive. He has done more than his full share of the work.

The uncertainty of performance is most marked when oral methods of teaching are largely employed. The history master, for example, may give an account of a war or of a movement to an interested class, and receive intelligent answers to his test questions. But when his boys are called upon shortly afterwards to write an essay on the subject of the lesson, they show lamentable ignorance and lack of power. Their apparent success during the oral lesson was due to the master's brain and not to their brains. He himself suggested the correct answers by the manner and circumstances of his questions. Deprived of his guidance the boys are at a loss. When teaching Latin on the direct method to beginners I have often been pleased by the amount of ground covered in the first month, by the extent to which the master was understood when he spoke Latin, and by the accuracy of the Latin answers given to his questions in that language. Then came a rude awakening. Left to do a simple piece of work by themselves, the class would make a mess of it. The correct performance of the preceding weeks had been due to the efforts of the teacher.

Learning is a matter of both understanding and of habituation. The former is generally not a difficult matter, the latter is both difficult and liable to be tedious. Good technique is chiefly occupied with unobtrusive insistence that the repeated action necessary for the formation of a new habit should be performed correctly by the boys without their becoming bored or weary.

It is practice that makes perfect; by doing a thing carefully and often we learn how to do it well. This truism enables us to put the essence of good technique into a few simple rules.

(1) The teacher should speak and do as little as possible. His business is to make the learner work rather than to work himself. His energies will be taxed enough in giving guidance, in keeping touch with the working of the boys' minds, and in seeing that the weaker brethren of the class are making extra efforts. He cannot do his own duty properly if he does the learners' work as well as his own.

This rule condemns at once all excessive use of lectures, and requires the teacher to exercise the greatest possible care in putting questions and in estimating progress from the answers he receives.

(2) As what we learn for ourselves is better known than what we are taught by others, the good teacher will gradually increase the element of research in his scholar's activities. The correct use of text-books and of books of reference will be taught at the earliest possible moment in a boy's career, and a request for information will often be answered by a hint to "look it up." The arts and the experimental sciences are better

taught than are the humanities just because the necessity of self-help is much more obvious in the case of the former. Even the most stupid boy understands that he cannot be told how to paint, in the sense that he can be told that the battle of Hastings was fought in 1066.

(3) The best way to learn is to teach others. As soon as we know a thing fairly well, to attempt to explain it to somebody else is the best way to fix our knowledge so that it becomes part and parcel of our mental equipment. Good technique will welcome any means whereby a learner is turned for the nonce into a teacher and the teacher acts as a kind of chairman.

If the teacher reduces his lectures to a minimum and increases the amount of exposition assigned to pupils, he will do much to realise the ideal of education as enlightened self-discipline. The responsibility of learning is thrown upon the learner, with a proportional gain in self-respect and self-confidence. The pupil realises that he has a part to play, and self-respect will tell him that he must play it well.

The question of lectures is of such outstanding importance that a more detailed discussion may be useful. Schoolmasters very rarely lecture for a whole period to a class of boys, but a practically unbroken exposition of twenty minutes is by no means uncommon, and in any case the master is on the whole heard far too much. A stopwatch would reveal some surprising truths. As the pupil gets older, the more lectures he hears, and at the University the lecture system has been adopted as the staple method[1] of instruction.

Now the utmost that a lecture can do is to supply material, and, in a few exceptional cases, to inspire the audience with enthusiasm. As Plato saw, it is easier for the lecturer to be pleasingly persuasive than to put his hearers on the road to knowledge, and most undergraduates flock to an amusing speaker and desert those who fail to entertain them. Again, the contact between the teacher and the taught is slight and uncertain. The lecturer can only guess whether his exposition is above or below their comprehension; in fact he often feels obliged to confine his remarks to supplementing the deficiencies of text-books and bringing them up to date. The learner, on his side, is entirely uncontrolled. He receives from a lecture just as much as he is able and willing to receive. At the best his progress is in passive knowledge only. He gets no practice in expressing himself, and performance—and performance alone—educates the mind, just as in painting, music, and the arts generally, it educates the hand.

These remarks are based upon the facts of

[1] That there are classes, "supervision," and papers, in addition to lectures, does not disprove the contention that far too much is expected from the lecture system.

University lecturing because the inherent defects of this method of instruction are most obvious in undergraduate education, but the less formal and shorter lectures of schoolmasters are open to the same objection. Of course, the lecture has its uses, even for schoolboys, but its function is a narrow one, and it should play but a small part in any educational scheme. It is hard not to believe that reasons of economy—the advantages of a lecture, such as they are, may be enjoyed by all those to whom the lecturer is audible—do not account for the strong hold the present system has upon our Universities. It must also be remembered that the lecture affords none of the stimulus given by the conditions of the school class-room.

But the school-boy can be trained to give continuous expositions; that is to say, he can take the place of the teacher, who becomes an umpire while the rest of the class are critics. The preparation of his discourse gives the boy practice in the use of text-books with perhaps the opportunity of doing a little research; its delivery is an exercise in English, in logical expression of thought, in elocution, and in control of nervousness. Of course a boy can have a whole lesson assigned to him only once or twice in a term, but several times a week each member of a class might have a chance of expressing his new knowledge in the form of a continuous speech. Boys can hold debates, solve mathematical problems, conduct scientific experiments, give exhibitions of drawing on the black-board—in fact they can do all, or nearly all, that the masters do. The interest of this method and the keen delight shown in it by the boys are additional advantages, to say nothing of the outstanding merit that the work is being done by the learners themselves, either as performers or as critics, while the master's energies are free to guide, to suggest, to apportion praise or blame, and to watch each individual in the class. The idea of the boys becoming in turn master, or at least "holding the stage" for a great part of the school hours, is no theoretic novelty, but has been tried at the Perse School, Cambridge. Of course, new material can be presented only by the master himself or through the use of a text-book, and to the boys must be assigned revision and practice. Incidentally, far more attention ought to be paid to training boys to use text-books and books of reference. To do so quickly and efficiently is an art which is seldom explained to boys. Yet their lack of skill in this respect is surprising, and they often go up to the University quite unprepared for a course one half at least of which must consist of private study. As far as my personal experience goes, only about one candidate for honours out of every three can be trusted to master unaided a text-book, even one on a sub-

ject with which he is already fairly familiar. Of
the pass candidates very few indeed could successfully satisfy this test. To read is not necessarily
to understand, and to understand is not necessarily to learn. The active process of expressing
in one's own words what has recently been
studied must be habitual. At first this *précis*
should be in writing, but as time goes on and
the habit grows stronger, the mind will carry
out the process by itself, subconsciously and
without effort. When one can repeat a thing with
accuracy and certainty, adding perhaps a little
of one's originality to the performance, the result
being not a mere effort of memory but an expression of one's personality, then and then only
is the knowledge, I do not say complete, but
satisfactory. All this may seem a truism, yet how
often is the undergraduate satisfied with verbally
memorising his lecture-notes!

The principle of making the learner an in-
structor is one which can be applied to University studies even more easily than in schools,
and perhaps with more important results. Papers
can be read frequently, demonstrations given by
pupils, and lectures reduced to a minimum. The
number of lectures necessary will of course vary
with the various subjects, but one a day in most
cases is quite enough. The small class should
replace the lecture, and the general principle be
faithfully observed of the student's expressing

in his own language all that he learns, and of learning as much as possible by his own unaided, though not unguided, efforts. Action ought to take precedence over passive listening. There will be an increase in the cost, but it will be compensated for by a more than proportional increase in attainment and efficiency.

NOTE. A friendly critic has maintained:

(1) that the pupils at a lecture, although not engaged in self-expression, are not passive but react to the lecture;

(2) that the method of making pupils take the part of lecturer or master can only apply to post-graduate work.

In reply to (1) I would point out that the reaction referred to does not include certain factors that are essential for all true education, and that it is a fatal error to attach too much importance to it, as is done when lectures are made the basis of education.

As regards (2) I can only say that I have seen pupils of all ages from 12 upwards take the part of master with success and thorough enjoyment. The practice was an integral part of the method adopted at the Perse while I was a master there.

## Conclusion

I HAVE now discussed my thesis from many educational points of view. Several lines of evidence lead to the conclusion that interest, in the narrow sense of a liking for a particular subject, however valuable it may be as a subsidiary motive, is an unsound basis upon which to build up an educational system. For the maxim "Effort through interest" should be substituted the maxim "Intelligent self-discipline for the sake of an ideal purpose." Submission to law, united to a fighting spirit, is a necessary condition without which this purpose cannot be attained, whether it be the rudimentary purpose of pleasing one's educators or the higher purpose of realising the ideal self. Active self-expression should be more insisted on, both in order to foster good mental and physical habits and also in order to encourage the learner by the joy of successful performance. Men should be chosen for the teaching profession who have the gift of leadership and the power to influence boys, even though the financial inducement necessary to secure them would mean less expensive buildings, equipment, and organisation.

# SHORT BIBLIOGRAPHY

The conclusions reached in this little work are entirely the result of personal experience. But a few books are here given which deal with the same subject.

1907 *Suggestion in Education*, by M. W. Keatinge. (Black.)

1909 *Principles and Methods of Moral Training with special reference to School Discipline*, by J. Welton and F. G. Blandford. (Clive.)

1909 *Habit Formation and the Science of Teaching*, by Stuart H. Rowe. (Longmans.)

1909 *How we Think*, by J. Dewey. (Heath.)

1910 *The Teaching of Scientific Method*, by Henry E. Armstrong. (Macmillan.)

1910 *Educational Essays*, by John Dewey, edited by J. J. Findlay, pp. 73–132: *Interest in relation to the Training of the Will*. (Blackie.)

1911 *What is and what might be*, by E. Holmes. (Constable.)

1912 *Instinct and Experience*, by C. Lloyd Morgan. (Methuen.)

1912 *The Adolescent*, by J. W. Slaughter. (Allen & Unwin.)

1915 *Educational Values and Methods*, by W. G. Sleight. (Oxford University Press.)

1916 *Studies in Education*, by M. W. Keatinge. (Black.)

1916 *Mechanisms of Character Formation*, by W. A. White. (Macmillan.)

1917 *The Play Way*, by H. Caldwell Cook. (Heinemann.)

1917 *The State and the Child*, by Clarke Hall. (Headley.)

1919 *Experimental Education*, by Robert R. Rusk. (Longmans.)

1920 *Educational Experiments in England*, by Alice Woods. (Methuen.)

1922 *An Introduction to the Psychology of Education*, by James Drever. (Arnold.)

1925 *Educational Psychology*, by Charles Fox. (Kegan Paul.)

Printed in the United States
By Bookmasters